HEADLINE ISSUES

Energy for the Future

Angela Royston

Heinemann
LIBRARY

Heinemann Library is an imprint of Capstone Global Library Limited, a company incorporated in England and Wales having its registered office at 7 Pilgrim Street, London, EC4V 6LB - Registered company number: 6695582

"Heinemann" is a registered trademark of Pearson Education Limited, under licence to Capstone Global Library Limited

Text © Capstone Global Library Limited 2009
First published in hardback in 2009
The moral rights of the proprietor have been asserted.

Edited by Sarah Eason and Leon Gray
Designed by Calcium and Geoff Ward
Original illustrations © Capstone Global Library Limited 2009
Illustrated by Geoff Ward
Picture research by Maria Joannou
Originated by Heinemann Library
Printed and bound in China by CTPS

ISBN 978 0 431162 75 1 (hardback)
13 12 11 10 09
10 9 8 7 6 5 4 3 2 1

British Library Cataloguing in Publication Data
Royston, Angela
 Energy for the future. - (Headline issues)
 1. Energy development - Juvenile literature 2. Power resources - Research - Juvenile literature
 I. Title
 333.7'9
A full catalogue record for this book is available from the British Library.

Acknowledgements
We would like to thank the following for permission to reproduce photographs:
Alamy Images: Imagebroker 17t, SpatzPhoto 28; Corbis: Boyd & Evans 27b, Kheled El Fiqi/EPA 18b, Victor Tonelli/Reuters 15, George Steinmetz 8b; Dreamstime: Braendan 18–19, Gillies11 29, Iofoto 7; Fotolia: Nicolas Berthy 13t, Eric Gevaert 20–21; Getty: AFP 25b, Popperfoto 23; Istockphoto: Ian Hamilton 26–27, 27t, Dale Taylor 14–15, Lisa Vanovitch 13; Rex Features: Action Press 22b, EDPPICS/James Bass 11, Sari Gustafsson 13b; Shutterstock: 3, Stefan Ataman 20, Atanas.dk 4, Galyna Andrushko 9t, Algis Balezentis 16, Ian Bracegirdle 5t, Dainis Derics 26, Markus Gann 9b, Gary718 5, Risteski Goce 20, Joe Gough 12, Greenland 28–29, Péter Gudella 17, Brian A. Jackson 10–11, Emin Kuliyev 30–31, John Lock 15, Tobias Machhaus 1, 8–9, 8, Carlos E. Santa Maria 18, Petr Nad 14, Anja Peternelj 6, QiLux 24, Otmar Smit 32, Stephen Strathdee 21, Charles Taylor 24–25, Terekhov Igor 5b, TheSupe87 4, Tiggy Gallery 22, Kheng Guan Toh 19b, Don Tran 17b, Vladi 25t, Jerry Zitterman 10, Peter Zurek 7r; Wikipedia Commons: Claus Ableiter 22-23.

Cover photograph reproduced with permission of Alamy Images/Sean Sprague.

Every effort has been made to contact copyright holders of material reproduced in this book. Any omissions will be rectified in subsequent printings if notice is given to the publishers.

Contents

Some words are printed in bold, **like this**. You can find out what they mean by looking in the glossary on page 30.

Hooked on fossil fuel

Almost all of the world's **energy** comes from burning **coal, oil,** and **natural gas**. These three sources of energy are called **fossil fuels**. At the moment, people in rich countries cannot manage without fossil fuels. We burn these fuels to **generate** the electricity that lights up our rooms and runs electric machines. Oil is burned as a fuel for aeroplanes, cars, and trucks and to make plastics. At home, people burn natural gas for heating and for cooking.

Coal and oil

Until around 150 years ago, people used very little fossil fuels. They burned wood for heat and they travelled on horseback or walked. People began to burn large amounts of coal when **steam engines** were invented. Steam engines pulled trains and powered machines in factories. By the 1870s, coal was being used to generate electricity. In 1859, the first oil was drilled.

Petrol-driven cars were invented shortly afterwards. By 1910, oil was fuelling cars, trucks, and the first aeroplanes.

How fossil fuels formed

Coal, oil, and natural gas are called fossil fuels because they were formed millions of years ago. They formed when the remains of plants and sea animals became trapped between layers of rock. The weight of the rock pressing on these remains turned them into coal, oil, and natural gas.

Electric lights use about one-third of all the electricity generated from burning fossil fuels.

FACT!

◆ Burning fossil fuels provides more than 80 per cent of the world's energy supply.

◆ Every year, countries around the world burn 6,000 million tonnes (6,666 million tons) of coal to generate electricity.

BEHIND THE HEADLINES
Generating electricity

Electricity is generated in a **power station**. Some power stations burn coal to heat water and make steam. The steam turns a huge **turbine**, which turns the **generator**. Other power stations burn oil or gas to generate steam to turn the turbine. Some other power stations do not burn fossil fuels. A **hydroelectric power (HEP)** station uses running water to turn the turbine.

Smoke rises from the chimneys of a power station in Britain. The power station burns coal to generate electricity.

There are more cars on the road than ever before. Most run on petrol or diesel, which are both made from oil.

Trouble ahead

MANY PEOPLE ARE worried because **fossil fuels** will eventually run out. However, burning fossil fuels is causing a bigger problem – it is making the average temperature of the Earth's surface warmer. This is called **global warming**.

Fossil fuels cause global warming

High in the atmosphere, **carbon dioxide** traps heat from the Sun in much the same way that glass traps heat in a greenhouse. Carbon dioxide is the main **greenhouse gas**. This greenhouse effect keeps the Earth at temperatures we are used to. When we burn fossil fuels, they produce lots more carbon dioxide. The greenhouse works too well and the Earth gets much hotter.

Climate change

Global warming is already causing disasters around the world. It is producing **climate change** – serious and unexpected changes in the **climate** in different parts of the world. Many dry places, such as Australia, are becoming much drier. They may soon be too dry to grow crops.

As the Earth gets warmer, the thick layer of ice around the North and South poles is starting to melt. Warmer seas and all the extra water from melted ice will make the sea level rise. To slow down global warming, people need to stop burning so much fossil fuel.

Changing our ways

The great news is that scientists have already invented new ways of generating electricity without burning fossil fuels, such as **solar power stations** and **wind turbines**. Scientists are also looking to develop new ways of powering vehicles.

heat trapped by greenhouse gases

escaping heat

gases in the Earth's atmosphere

The Sun's heat warms the Earth. Some of the heat escapes back into space. Some is trapped by greenhouse gases and keeps the Earth warm.

ON THE SPOT
Maldives

The Maldives are a group of 1,200 small islands in the Indian Ocean. Tourists love the sandy beaches and warm seas. Most of the land lies between 1.5 and 2 metres (4.9 and 6.6 feet) above sea level. The islanders have built a high wall around Male, the capital. The wall keeps out waves, but it will not stop the islands from being flooded as the sea rises. In 100 years, most of the Maldives may be lost beneath the sea.

Rising sea levels may cause the Maldives to disappear for ever.

Solar energy for everyone

EVERY DAY VAST amounts of **energy** reach the Earth from the Sun. We can use both the Sun's light and heat to **generate** electricity. This is called "clean" energy, because it does not produce any **carbon dioxide**. Scientists have invented different ways of using energy from the Sun.

Solar panels

Two different kinds of **solar panels** can supply energy to buildings. One kind uses heat from the Sun to heat water for baths and showers. The other kind is a **photovoltaic (PV)** panel. It uses sunlight to generate electricity. At the moment, PV panels are expensive, but they will become cheaper. However, they do not work at night when electricity is most needed. Each panel only makes a small amount of electricity.

Solar power stations

A **solar power station** uses the Sun's heat to generate electricity. It uses curved mirrors to collect and concentrate the Sun's heat. The heat produces steam that drives a **turbine**. Solar power stations work well in deserts, where the Sun shines strongly all day. Some solar power stations store extra heat during the day so they can go on generating electricity at night. Others work alongside a second power station that burns **natural gas** at night.

Mirrors at a solar power station in California in the United States.

FACT!

✦ In one minute, the Earth gets enough energy from sunlight to meet the world's energy needs for one year.
✦ The Sun will keep shining for about another 5,000,000,000 years.

ON THE SPOT
Sahara Desert

The Sahara Desert is an empty desert, but one day these hot lands could supply clean electricity to the whole of Europe. One scheme plans to use around 100 solar power stations to generate one-sixth of Europe's electricity. At the same time, the power stations would turn saltwater into freshwater to **irrigate** crops.

The scorching heat of the Sahara Desert may be a future form of "clean energy" for Europe.

This roof is covered with photovoltaic panels. The panels use energy from the Sun to generate electricity.

Wind makes a comeback

IN THE PAST, people used windmills to grind corn. Today, windmills are making a comeback. They are starting to appear on hilltops, in fields, at sea, and on roof tops. These new types of windmills are called **wind turbines**.

Catching the wind

Wind turbines catch the wind to **generate** electricity. The blades of the turbines start to spin. The movement of the blades generates electricity. Once the wind turbines are built, they do not produce any **carbon dioxide**. As a result, wind turbines are helping to slow down **global warming**.

Windy places

One disadvantage of wind turbines is that they only generate electricity when there is enough wind. Therefore, it is best to build them where there is a strong, steady wind all year round. Hilltops and flat plains are windy, but the best place to build wind turbines is in the sea or in windy lakes. Bigger turbines can be built there, and they generate more electricity. Small turbines are used to generate electricity on yachts. Some people are building them on the roofs of their houses. Roof-top turbines only work well if the building is in a windy place.

Tidal turbines

Energy can also be generated by the movement of seawater. **Tidal turbines** work in a similar way to wind turbines, but they are underwater. The movement of seawater turns the blades. The main advantage of tidal turbines is that the tide never stops moving the water, and they generate electricity all the time. Like wind turbines, they do not produce any carbon dioxide and so they help to slow down global warming.

FACT!

✦ The blades of the biggest wind turbines can be up to 100 metres (333 feet) long.
✦ The largest wind farm in the world so far is in Texas in the United States. It has 421 turbines.

Wind turbines waste money: Who is right and who is wrong?

FOR

Wind turbines produce only a small amount of electricity. They spoil the scenery, and they are dangerous to birds, which get killed by the blades.

A wind farm is a group of wind turbines. This offshore wind farm has been built in the North Sea.

AGAINST

Large wind turbines produce a lot of electricity. Some people do not like them only because they are not used to them. There are ways to stop birds from being killed by them. We need more wind turbines to combat **climate change**.

Underfloor heating with a difference

DEEP BENEATH THE ground, hundreds of kilometres below the Earth's surface, the rocks are so hot they are molten. This means they are beginning to melt. A **geothermal power station** uses the heat of the molten rocks to **generate** electricity.

A **heat pump** does not need hot rocks to generate electricity. Instead it relies on the temperature difference between the surface of the ground and just a few metres below the surface. Sometimes the temperature at the surface is hotter than the temperature under the ground. Sometimes the temperature at the surface is much cooler. However, the temperature difference is always between 10 and 20°C (50 and 68°F).

Heat pumps

In the future, heat pumps that heat and cool individual buildings could become more common. Heat pumps are already used to control the temperature of the building that houses the Welsh Assembly in Swansea, Wales, and in buildings in many other countries.

In the winter, cold water is pumped through pipes into the warmer ground below the surface. The water warms up and is then used to heat up radiators inside the Welsh Assembly building. In the summer, water warmed by the building is pumped through pipes to the cooler ground below. Heat is taken away from the building, which makes it much cooler.

Geothermal power

In some parts of the world, molten rock rises up and comes very close to the Earth's surface. These are the best places to build geothermal power stations.

The water in a geothermal power station is heated by pumping it through the molten rock. This produces hot water or steam, which drives a **turbine** to generate electricity. Iceland, Italy, New Zealand, and California in the United States all have geothermal power stations. The only drawback to geothermal power is that the power stations can only be built in places where the molten rock rises near to the surface.

ON THE SPOT
Iceland

Reykjavik

Iceland lies very close to the Arctic Circle and is one of the coldest countries in the world. The country has a supply of hot water all year round in the form of **geysers**. These free supplies of hot water are used to heat almost all the buildings in the country. Long pipes carry the heated water to the capital, called Reykjavik.

The water from this geyser in Iceland is heated by molten rock just below the Earth's surface. The geyser provides a free supply of hot water. It pumps only steam into the air, and produces no greenhouse gases.

This geothermal power plant in Hellisheidarvirkjun supplies electricity to more than 60 per cent of the population of Iceland.

Is nuclear power the answer?

NUCLEAR POWER GETS vast amounts of **energy** from tiny particles called **atoms**. Every solid, liquid, and gas is made up of atoms. However, the atoms of a metal called uranium are special.

Uranium: Good or bad?

Uranium atoms break up very easily to form new atoms. As they do this, they produce heat. **Nuclear power stations** use this heat to **generate** electricity. Yet nuclear power stations cause other problems.

The main problem is that uranium is **radioactive**. This means that the uranium atoms produce a form of energy that can damage living things. The nuclear power station also produces radioactive waste. Storing radioactive waste is expensive and dangerous. If there is a leak, the radiation can kill people and other living things.

Nuclear fusion

When atoms break apart, the reaction is called **nuclear fission**. When they join up it is called **nuclear fusion**. Fusion produces lots of energy with less radioactivity. Two **hydrogen** atoms fuse (join) to create an atom of helium. The problem is that fusion only happens at very hot temperatures. Scientists have managed to fuse atoms in temperatures that are ten times hotter than the Sun. However, it may take 50 to 100 years before they will be able to build a nuclear fusion power station.

Nuclear power could be the solution to the energy crisis but many people are worried about its safety.

FACT!

✦ Nuclear waste can remain radioactive for thousands of years.
✦ The first use of nuclear fission was in the atom bombs dropped on Japan in 1945.

We should build more nuclear power stations: Who is right and who is wrong?

FOR

We need more nuclear power stations to replace the power stations that burn **fossil fuels**. We need them to combat **climate change**. Solar power and wind power will never produce enough electricity for the needs of everyone on the planet.

People in France protest against plutonium nuclear waste being transported from the United States into France.

AGAINST

No one has the right to create deadly nuclear waste that can harm people now and for thousands of years to come. We would not have to generate as much electricity if we did not waste so much in the first place.

Cleaner coal, cleaner air

As well as developing new ways to **generate** electricity, scientists are also trying to find ways to clean up **fossil fuels** and make **power stations** less wasteful.

Carbon pollution

There is enough **coal** left to supply the world for at least another one hundred years. The problem is that burning coal produces harmful **greenhouse gases**. Scientists have found ways to clean up the coal before it is burned. They can get rid of some of the substances that cause pollution. However, cleaning coal does not get rid of all these substances.

Capturing carbon

Scientists have also developed a way of catching the **carbon dioxide** before it escapes into the atmosphere. The carbon dioxide is cooled until it becomes liquid. The liquid is then stored deep in the ground. The problem is that the whole system costs a lot of money.

Wasting energy

Big power stations waste about three-quarters of the **energy** that is stored in fossil fuels. Nearly two-thirds of this wasted energy is lost as heat. The rest is lost as the electricity travels along cables to towns and cities.

Local power

Small power stations that supply local communities waste much less energy. Less energy is lost through cables because the electricity does not have to travel as far. Instead of wasting heat, these power stations reuse steam to heat water. The hot water is then piped to nearby buildings. These power stations are called Combined Heat and Power (CHP) stations.

FACT!
- Carbon capture and storage stops 80 per cent of carbon reaching the atmosphere.
- CHP stations can burn different fuels, including household rubbish.

This small power station in Denmark wastes very little energy. It supplies the local town with hot water and electricity.

BEHIND THE HEADLINES

Electricity grid

Huge electric pylons carry electricity to towns and cities.

Most countries use a grid system to supply people with electricity. The electricity from each power station goes into a network of electric cables that supplies the whole country. The system makes it easier to cope with changes in the demand for electricity in different places at different times.

Clean fuel for cars causes problems

Scientists are trying to replace petrol and **diesel** with cleaner fuels. **Biofuels** are made from plants. Ethanol is a biofuel that is made from crops such as sugar cane and wheat. **Biodiesel** is made from many vegetables such as palm seeds and soy beans. Governments in Asia, Europe, and the United States have encouraged farmers to grow crops for biofuels, because they are cleaner than burning **fossil fuels**. However, biofuels are causing other problems.

Food crisis

In Europe and North America, many farmers started to grow crops for biofuels instead of food crops. That meant that fewer crops for food were grown worldwide. This led to a shortage of food. A year or two later, the shortage caused the world price of food to more than double. In 2008, poor people in many countries could no longer afford to buy basic foods such as bread and rice. In June 2008, the European Union abandoned plans to replace more petrol with biofuels such as ethanol.

Cutting down the rainforests

Millions of tonnes of **carbon dioxide** are taken in and stored by **rainforests**. In this way the rainforests help to slow down **global warming**. Farmers in Asia are cutting down the trees in rainforests to grow crops to make biofuels. These plants take in much less carbon dioxide than the trees and are cut down after a few years.

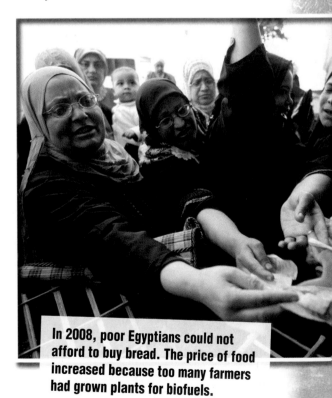

In 2008, poor Egyptians could not afford to buy bread. The price of food increased because too many farmers had grown plants for biofuels.

BEHIND THE HEADLINES
Carbon stores

Plants take in carbon dioxide from the air and use it to make food for new growth. The plants store the carbon as they grow. When they die, the carbon returns to the air as carbon dioxide.

This is the carbon cycle. Fossil fuels also store carbon. They contain carbon from the remains of plants and sea animals that lived millions of years ago. Burning fossil fuels releases this stored carbon.

These palm oil trees are growing on land that used to be rainforest. Palm oil seeds are used to make biofuels.

Hybrids take to the road

Vehicles of the future will use much less petrol and **diesel**. Some will use none at all. Electric motors run on electricity. They make much less **carbon dioxide** than engines that run on petrol.

Electric cars

Electric cars produce no **exhaust fumes** and so they do not pollute the air. However, most electric cars get their power from heavy **batteries**. Even the most powerful batteries have to be recharged every few hundred kilometres. They are recharged by plugging them directly into the electricity grid.

Some people already drive hybrid cars, but they are expensive to buy.

Most electricity is made by burning **fossil fuels**, so recharging batteries produces carbon dioxide.

Hybrid cars

Some cars are cleaner than other cars because they use less petrol. **Hybrid cars** are one example. They use a small petrol engine and an electric motor. The electric motor provides extra power when it is needed. The batteries that power the electric motor recharge themselves every time the car brakes or slows down.

No solution for aircraft

Aircraft produce more carbon dioxide than any other form of transport. So far, no clean fuel provides enough power to fly an aeroplane. Flying is also becoming more popular. Air travel is cheap because airlines do not pay tax on fuel, even though all other vehicles have to pay a fuel tax.

FACT!

✦ When petrol prices rose by 15 per cent in Britain in 2008, people reduced the petrol they used by about 25 per cent by driving more carefully and making fewer journeys.
✦ Hybrid cars use one-quarter of the amount of fuel compared to most four-wheel drive cars.

Air travellers should pay fuel tax: Who is right and who is wrong?

FOR

Air travel **generates** more **greenhouse gases** than any other way of travelling. People should be charged for their share of these greenhouse gases.

Aeroplanes need powerful engines for take off, and they burn large amounts of fuel.

AGAINST

Higher fuel taxes would mean that only the rich could afford to fly. In addition, every country would have to agree to the same rate of tax.

Hydrogen – the ultimate solution?

HYDROGEN FUEL CELLS might save the world from **global warming**. One day we could be using **hydrogen fuel cells** to power our buses and cars and to **generate** electricity for our homes. However, that day could be decades away.

What is a fuel cell?

A fuel cell is similar to a **battery**, because it stores electricity. A fuel cell combines hydrogen with oxygen to make electricity and heat. The only waste the fuel cell produces is water. The cleanest way to produce hydrogen is to split water into oxygen and hydrogen, but that uses electricity!

In the future, scientists plan to use electricity made by solar cells to produce the hydrogen. Fuel cells could then replace car engines and central heating boilers.

World of hydrogen

The change from petrol to hydrogen fuel cells has already begun. Many cities, including Vancouver in Canada and London in Britain, operate buses that run on the new power source. These buses carry gas cylinders instead of petrol tanks. Before hydrogen can take over from petrol, however, hydrogen stations have to be built along every highway. Norway and California in the United States have started to build these hydrogen highways.

This bus in Hamburg in Germany gets its power from hydrogen fuel cells.

BEHIND THE HEADLINES
Is hydrogen safe?

Burning hydrogen is less dangerous than burning petrol, but many people are scared of hydrogen fuel. One of the main reasons is a disaster that happened more than 70 years ago. The *Hindenburg* was an **airship** that carried passengers below a huge hydrogen-filled balloon. In May 1937, the airship flew across the Atlantic Ocean and landed in New Jersey. As it did so, the airship caught fire and exploded. Of the 97 people on board, 35 of them died. People think that most of the victims burned to death, but most of them died when they tried to escape the flames by jumping to the ground.

The *Hindenburg* airship caught fire on 6 May 1937, while it was trying to dock with its mooring mast at an air station in New Jersey, USA.

Better than batteries

Billions of batteries are used every year, but they could soon become a thing of the past. As mobile phones, lap-top computers, and other electronic devices become more complex, they will need more power to work properly. Disposable batteries would soon run out, and rechargeable batteries would need constantly recharging. **Fuel cells** and solar cells can supply much more electricity than disposable or rechargeable batteries.

Micro fuel cells

A tiny fuel cell is called a **micro fuel cell**. Some companies are developing micro fuel cells to provide power for electronic devices, such as mobile phones. They use cartridges of **hydrogen**, methanol, or ethanol as the fuel, but they have to be replaced or refilled to keep the cells working properly.

Producing the cartridges, and using methanol or ethanol, still produces **greenhouse gases**. In the future, micro fuel cells that use hydrogen could be recharged simply by topping them up with water.

Solar chargers

Solar cells convert the energy from the Sun into electricity. Some companies already produce solar chargers. These devices open up during the day to collect sunlight and **generate** electricity to recharge batteries. Although solar chargers are slow and inefficient, they create no greenhouse gases and can be used even when there is no power plug nearby.

No charger needed

Solar cells are already used to power some electronic calculators. Solar cells never run out and they do not need to be recharged. However, scientists and engineers have found it difficult to get enough power from solar cells to run more complex equipment.

However, one company is designing a stack of solar cells behind a touch screen. The company hopes that the stack of solar cells will provide enough power to run a mobile phone combined with an MP3 player. The device will be recharged simply by leaving it in the sunlight.

BEHIND THE HEADLINES
Rechargeable batteries

Most rechargeable batteries last around five years. This is much longer than disposable batteries. Rechargeable batteries contain cadmium, which is a poisonous metal. When they are thrown away, rechargeable batteries can sometimes leak and damage the environment. Also, the rechargeable batteries produce greenhouse gases when they are recharged with electricity made by burning **fossil fuels**.

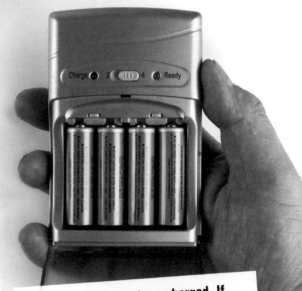

These batteries can be recharged. If the electricity used to recharge them is generated by burning fossil fuels, they will add to global warming.

This mobile phone gets its power from a small hydrogen fuel cell.

Eco-homes make no carbon

THE BUILDINGS OF the future will need to save much more **energy** to combat **climate change**. This will help to reduce **greenhouse gases** *and* save money. They will be built in ways that reduce energy use. They might use solar or wind power to **generate** electricity.

Eco-homes

Eco-homes are designed to use up as little electricity as possible. For example, they have no central heating or air conditioning. Instead the windows of these houses face the Sun so that it heats the rooms. No heat escapes because the walls and roof are insulated. In summer, the rooms are shaded to keep them cool. Eco-homes recycle water and kitchen waste, too.

Cutting carbon

People can make changes so their homes produce less **carbon dioxide**.

One simple way to do this is to change from traditional light bulbs to CFL (compact **fluorescent lamp**) bulbs.

CFL bulbs use about one-fifth as much electricity as traditional light bulbs. CFL bulbs also last more than eight times as long. Amazingly, most homes waste almost one-third of the electricity they use and pay for. So an even simpler way of cutting carbon dioxide is to stop wasting electricity! Page 29 tells you how to do this.

These homes have wind-catchers on their roofs. The wind-catchers pull in cool air so that the buildings do not need air conditioning.

✦ Turning down the central heating by 1.5°C (2.7°F) saves 1 tonne (1.1 tons) of carbon dioxide a year.
✦ One-quarter of the heat in many houses is lost through an uninsulated roof.

ON THE SPOT
Taos, New Mexico

In the desert just north of Taos is a village of 130 houses. The houses are no ordinary houses – they are "earthships" that produce no carbon dioxide. They are built of earth and recycled materials, such as old car tyres and glass bottles. They have **solar panels** and **wind turbines** to generate electricity. They each collect and recycle their own water.

This is Earthship 1, one of the 130 houses in the desert of New Mexico, USA.

Get involved!

EVERYONE HAS TO work together to slow down **global warming**. Governments need to build **power stations** that do not burn **fossil fuels**. Businesses and other organizations need to change the way they do things too.

Offices and factories produce less **carbon dioxide**. Families, too, can help to fight the effects of global warming. Take a look around your home and school. Can you suggest any ways of saving **energy**?

Cycling saves burning petrol, and it is healthy, too.

THINGS TO DO

Turning off the lights when you leave a room saves electricity and reduces greenhouse gases.

Save electricity
- Turn off lights.
- Don't leave televisions and DVD players on stand-by.
- Put computers to "sleep" if you leave them for more than a few minutes.
- Unplug chargers for mobile phones and MP3 players when the recharging is finished.
- Open fridge and freezer doors for as short a time as possible.

Persuade your parents and school to:
- Replace traditional light bulbs with CFL light bulbs.
- Turn down the central heating when your home or school is empty.
- Turn off the air conditioning when the home or school is empty.
- Insulate the roof.
- Make windows draught-proof to stop heat from leaking out.
- Dry clothes on racks instead of using the tumble drier.

Save petrol
- Walk or cycle short distances instead of going by car.
- Take the bus or train for longer journeys instead of travelling by car.
- If you have to go by car, try to share lifts with your friends.

Persuade your parents to:
- Avoid flying unless it is absolutely necessary.
- Change their car for one that makes less carbon dioxide.
- Use less petrol by driving more slowly.
- Remove the roof-rack when it is not being used.
- Unload heavy things that don't need to be carried.

Glossary

airship lighter-than-air aircraft

atom minute "building block" that makes up all substances

battery device that supplies a limited amount of electricity

biodiesel type of diesel oil made from plants or waste materials

biofuel fuel made from plants such as palm oil seeds and sugar cane

carbon dioxide one of the gases in the air. Carbon dioxide traps the Sun's heat and so leads to global warming.

climate different kinds of weather that usually occur in a place at different times of the year

climate change unexpected changes to the weather caused by global warming

coal black solid found in the ground that is burned as a fuel

diesel fuel that is made from oil

energy power needed to make something move, or to produce heat

exhaust fume waste gas produced by an engine as it burns fuel

fluorescent lamp electric lamp that produces light without producing waste heat

fossil fuel fuel such as oil and gas that formed from the remains of plants and animals that lived millions of years ago

fuel cell device that generates electricity using oxygen and another gas such as hydrogen or methane

generate produce

generator machine with rotating parts that makes electricity

geothermal power electricity generated using heat from inside the Earth

geyser natural spring that shoots up columns of hot water and steam

global warming an increase in the average temperature at Earth's surface

greenhouse gas gas in the atmosphere that traps the Sun's heat

heat pump electric pump that moves hot air or liquid from one place to heat another place

hybrid car car that works by using a petrol engine and an electric motor

hydroelectric power (HEP) electricity generated by the force of running water

hydrogen invisible, odourless gas

irrigate supply dry land with water

micro fuel cell very small fuel cell

natural gas fossil fuel in the form of gas

nuclear fission splitting of atoms. Nuclear fission releases energy.

nuclear fusion joining together of two atoms to make a new atom. Nuclear fusion releases energy.

nuclear power electricity made by splitting atoms of uranium

oil fossil fuel in the form of a liquid

photovoltaic (PV) producing electricity when light falls on a particular substance

power station building in which electricity is generated

radioactive giving off a harmful form of energy

rainforest thick forest where it rains heavily almost every day

solar panel flat panel that generates electricity or heat when light shines on it

solar power station power station that generates electricity using the Sun's heat

steam engine engine that uses the force of steam to make something move

tidal turbine device that uses the movement of seawater caused by the tides to generate electricity

turbine engine that spins around to generate electricity

wind turbine turbine turned by wind to make electricity

Find out more

Books

Energy (Sustainable Futures), John Stringer (Evans Brothers Ltd, 2005)

Energy for the Future (Earth in Danger), Helen Orme (Bearport Publishing, 2008)

Energy of the Future (Eco-action), Angela Royston (Heinemann Library, 2008)

Energy Supplies (Action for the Environment), Chris Oxlade (Franklin Watts, 2006)

Energy Technology (New Technology), Chris Oxlade (Smart Apple Media, 2008)

Future Energy (Your Environment), Sally Morgan (Stargazer Books, 2005)

Saving Energy (Improving Our Environment), Jen Green (Hodder Wayland, 2005)

Websites

This informative website tells you all about fossil fuels and where they come from. Click on the links to find out about other ways of generating electricity.
http://home.clara.net/darvill/altenerg/fossil.htm

The U.S. Department of Energy website talks about renewable energy resources and explains how you can improve your energy efficiency. Play the games to test your energy knowledge at:
www.eere.energy.gov/kids

This website is run by the charity Planet 21. It looks at some of the key issues that face the world, such as climate change and renewable energy, and tells you what you can do to help.
www.peopleandplanet.net

Index